KEYS TO GENERATING SALES: Discover business strategies that sell

Edwardo Mendez

Table of Contents

Introduction

Everyone seems to have something they can sell, whether it is a service, a commodity, or some important knowledge.

Gaining clients and increasing revenues from that service, item, or piece of knowledge are the only ways a firm may prosper.

However, you can't simply sit back and hope that someone would come across your product and buy it.

Sales growth is the outcome of well-thought-out sales tactics that are designed and put into action. You may either expand the number of people you sell to, better the product you offer, enhance your message, or do all of the above to boost sales.

You can significantly boost sales if you can even slightly enhance each phase of your sales process.

Chapter 1

Business Sales Leads; How and why you should increase it

Increasing your sales leads is essential for growing your company's revenue. How to get more sales leads for your company is provided here.

Many successful businesses rely on expanding their clientele to expand their operations. Making ensuring that businesses obtain a consistent flow of sales leads is a crucial step in achieving this aim. Here are some strategies you may use to get leads for your company.

How crucial are sales leads are?

A sales lead is a potential customer for the products or services offered by your organization. Once you've determined a lead's degree of interest and suitability as a client for your company, a lead turns into a prospect. Advertising and marketing, cold calling, social media, referrals, outreach and networking, consultations, product/service trials, and other techniques may all be used to get sales leads.

Your company may generate a consistent flow of inbound sales leads with the aid of inbound marketing techniques. For your company to produce sales leads, use the following lead creation tactics.

1. **Request recommendations from existing clients.**

Because they have previously made a purchase from you and are aware of how well your goods and services perform, your existing customers may be your finest source of new business. As a result, they have to be an essential component of your plan to draw in fresh sales leads.

Warm recommendations are more effective than cold emails or an approach to uninterested prospects.

However, a lot of companies just follow up with previous clients to provide assistance or customer care when necessary after the transaction. They don't express gratitude to clients for their patronage, nor do they request recommendations or assistance in bringing in new clients.

These tactics may assist in converting existing clients into excellent sources of sales leads:

Ensure that consumers are happy with your goods or services and customer support by asking your account manager to check on this. Ask them to get in touch to discuss strategies to improve the issue.

Plan a brief dialogue with your client to express your appreciation for their business. Make sure they know how much you respect their connection, and talk about how you can make it even better.

Request the names and contact details of business associates or other organizations that may want your product or service, along with the details of why they would be a suitable match.

First, make a brief phone call or email to the prospect and ask your customer to reach out on your behalf. You may advise them on what to write in an email to convey the value you provide to the sales lead.

With a meaningful present, thank your customer for the recommendation. Instead of mentioning the company's goods and services, make it about you.

2. **Use your network to find potential customers.**

Everyone has a personal network of relatives, friends, and coworkers, as well as former and present business partners, neighbors, and service providers (such as plumbers, physicians, attorneys, and landscapers). For several reasons, you can neglect these individuals as potential sources of sales leads, but you need to consider them as one of your first choices. Since you already have their trust, you may use them to generate leads.

Although you are shared by the people in your network, many of them reside in other spheres of your life and don't engage with one another. Each individual can produce very important sales leads since they do not have the same connections. You might ask them to introduce you to prospects after having a conversation with them about your life and company.

How should you start the procedure? Just let them know you're searching. Describe the kind of person or company you want to connect with in detail. Describe their sector of the economy, size of the company, range of sales and revenues, and so on. Ask them to get in touch with the person on your behalf to make the introduction if they know someone. Even better, give them the email so they may send it to their contact.

Always keep in mind that you are interacting with a friend or acquaintance with who you want to remain in your network. If you mix your personal and work life, you must show consideration for their time and the connection.

3. **At networking events, interact with potential customers.**

Make visiting offline and online networking events a regular component of your lead generation process. A good technique to meet new people and strengthen connections with acquaintances you've already made is via networking. You may interact face-to-face with your leads as well.

Picking the right events is important since networking takes time. To make the most of this time, go to networking events where your sales leads are most likely to materialize. To get the most out of your networking, use the following tactics:

Building ties with actual people is a key component of networking. Instead of approaching individuals from a sales standpoint, enter the situation to first attempt to assist others. Learn about their company and them personally, then determine what they need to prosper or resolve an issue.

Give new individuals you meet business cards at in-person networking events. Include the individual's contact details in your customer relationship management system. Send an email to thank them for meeting you at the event the next week as a follow-up.

Inquire about LinkedIn connections at both offline and online networking events. Even if they transfer to a different company, it's a terrific method to keep in contact.
Enjoy yourself and be yourself.

4. **Go back and look at missed chances.**

The word "no" may also signify "not now."

You've undoubtedly contacted a lot of companies that weren't your customers at the time. Please make another contact. They are already aware of what your company does. You may have conducted a discovery call and maybe given a demonstration of your item or service. At the time, they didn't purchase, but that may change.

Reconsider missed or closed chances. Every four to six months, get in touch with the prospect again. As for their objectives, difficulties, ambitions, and demands in terms of their company, inquire whether anything has changed.

Sales prospects that have never purchased from you are already qualified. Spend time and money promoting these potential customers. Blog postings targeted messaging, and authorized marketing emails may help you stay in contact.

The next three times you contact them, you may not succeed in closing the deal. However, after the fourth, fifth, or sixth time they hear from you, you could obtain a sale or an interest. And there is no doubt that your prospect's circumstances will alter. It could become more feasible for them to acquire your solution on a tighter budget. Or your contact could change jobs or departments, where there will be a need or incentive to use your solution.

When it comes time for sales leads to choose their sales solution, being at the top of their minds will make you the first company they contact.

5. **Look for sales leads on relevant social media sites.**

Your sales leads are online, just like everyone else. You merely need to locate them and get in touch with them.

Use LinkedIn to produce high-caliber sales leads because you're presumably on there already (or you should be). On LinkedIn, you may find the specialty businesses and contacts you're looking for. They come here to do business, broaden their network, market their goods and services, and address their company's requirements.

Utilize the tactics below to use your social media presence to get new customers:

Connect with as many members of your current network as you can, in addition to sales prospects and business associates in your sector. Since you may now connect with your contacts, every link aids in extending your reach. Any relationship may be a source of quality sales leads; you don't even need to know your contacts personally.

Inform your network about your ideal clients and the kinds of issues you can assist them with. You may provide an update or create a post about what you're searching for at the moment. As an example, consider the following: "We're hoping to assist Denver-area dentists and orthodontists with increasing their advertising reach throughout the back-to-school season."

To show your worth and level of customer service, get referrals or

testimonials from two to three of your existing customers on the job you've completed for them.
These tactics are targeted towards LinkedIn. However, you may broaden the audience for your business and build your brand on other social media platforms that are appropriate for it, including Instagram, Facebook for Business, Twitter, Snapchat, and so on. Select the best social media platform for your company. Concentrate your efforts on the social media sites that will provide the most qualified sales leads.

6. **Make your social media accounts more appealing to the right kind of sales leads.**

You must update your social media profiles if you have any. You may generate more sales leads if you keep your LinkedIn, Twitter, Instagram, and other social media profiles up to date.

The objective is to draw customers' attention and facilitate connections.

Create a compelling title and description on LinkedIn that will appeal to your intended audience. What you do and who you serve should be stated in your headline and summary. Employ keywords that your intended customer would use while you concentrate on what they'll be searching for. For instance, your headline could be something like "Sales Manager | Creating Solutions for Human Resources Managers in the Automotive Industry" rather than "Sales Maven."

Twitter: Add a professional profile picture, a link to your LinkedIn account, and pertinent hashtags that would be important to your target audience in addition to your title and a link to your company's account. Follow Twitter users in your field and those who may be future

customers. For your account to remain active, retweet and comment.
Instagram is an extremely graphic social media tool. Include a professional picture, appealing and pertinent photographs, and hashtags that matter to potential customers. Be professional while yet having fun.

7. **Establish an email chain.**
A set of emails sent to recipients on a mailing list automatically becomes an email sequence. The purpose of email marketing is to increase recipients' interest in the goods and services offered by your business.

Email sequences may be of two primary types:

Trigger-based sequences deliver emails in response to a person doing a certain action, such as visiting a specific page on your website, making a purchase, joining your email list, or leaving an item in their shopping cart without making a purchase.

Time-based sequences send emails at predetermined intervals, such as two weeks after a transaction, right away after a newsletter opt-in, or on an anniversary.

Email sequences should be developed with a particular goal in mind to successfully acquire sales leads. The attention of the reader is increased with each email in the series by building on the one before it. You might, for instance, use the following pattern, with each email ending with a call to action (such as, "Click here for more information" or "Click here to buy this product"):

In your first email, introduce yourself and identify a typical problem that your reader could be experiencing.
Talk about the worth of your item or service in your second email.
Third email: Describe a customer's experience using your product or service to address an issue.
Fourth email: Outline your customer services.
Fifth email: List the advantages of utilizing your products or service.
Sixth email: Make contact once more and provide a unique offer.

8. **Create and post enlightening blogs and articles.**

Establishing your expertise in your subject via blog posts and articles might be helpful. Write about your expertise and how it might benefit others. The possibilities are unlimited, but you may start by offering advice on how to make other people more productive, save money, boost sales, enhance profits, expand their businesses, and so on.

You become a recognized expert via writing. People can read what you say and determine that you are knowledgeable in your field. Your expertise may inform readers, and they will come to you when they want to learn more or make a purchase based on what you've taught them.

Blogging is a component of a content marketing plan that may increase website traffic and assist with lead creation. You may increase website traffic and direct prospective customers to the landing page you want them to see by including content marketing in your lead generation plan.

You may include a call to action on that landing page to entice website visitors to find out more, make a purchase right away, or take any other action you want prospective leads to consider.

Articles and blog entries may be written and published in a variety of places:

your blog or website
a blog or website for your business
LinkedIn and other platforms for social networking
Additional business, sector, and individual blogs
websites that post blogs and articles for industries
websites of your clients
You may also post blogs and articles via an email newsletter. Additionally, this helps you establish connections with your target market. People are already interested in what you have to say since

they have to sign up to get the newsletter. They consent to you marketing to them as long as you enlighten, educate, or amuse them along the route.

9. **Conduct an online workshop or webinar.**

Writing blog posts and articles is a terrific way to educate others and share your expertise. They are, however, one-way discussions in which you write and another person reads. You may educate and communicate with people via webinars and online seminars, which can be more effective in generating leads for sales.

You may go into deeper detail when imparting your expertise to potential customers via webinars and online courses. You might utilize video and pictures to demonstrate each stage in the process of teaching someone how to develop a marketing campaign, for instance. Every participant in the webinar or workshop is a qualified sales lead. This method of imparting information to others positions you as a thought leader in your industry fosters trust and improves your capacity to get leads.

You may conduct live webinars and online seminars to answer inquiries immediately and develop time-limited live offers to pique the interest of sales prospects. Additionally, you may archive webinars and workshops to reach audiences around the clock and generate leads for sales even when you are not there. On the website of your business, you may offer webinars and online workshops; alternatively, you can develop these events and host them elsewhere.

10. **Interact with users of live chat.**
Thanks to machine learning and artificial intelligence, chat technology have advanced significantly. You may design a customized chatbot that is consistent with the appearance and feel of your company brand for your website. The chatbot may show up with a welcome message whenever someone enters your website.

Chapter 2

Getting In Touch With Customers

There are several methods to interact with clients, but which ones work best? Business owners, managers, and customer relationship specialists provide advice on how and where to interact most effectively with current and potential clients.

More avenues than ever before exist now to interact with consumers. Email, social media, mobile, gatherings, focus groups, and trade exhibitions are all available. The list continues. But which approaches work best?

Top suggestions for connecting with consumers are shown below, along with an explanation of why each one is successful.

A method's effectiveness is substantial, if not totally, dependent on the kind of company you are in and the nature of your clients. Although social media platforms like Facebook, Twitter, and YouTube may be ideal for certain businesses, they may not be the greatest choice for others. Similar to how some clients would prefer email engagement, others might prefer or value a phone conversation or in-person encounter.

Ask your consumers how they want to be contacted or engaged before you spend too much time or money on one specific kind of client outreach. Regarding potential clients, every expert we spoke with advised businesses to experiment with various types of outreach and determine which ones were most effective.

- **Question your clients**

Businesses may immediately determine consumer demands via surveys.
Companies may direct their services toward meeting these objectives once consumers' wants are established, he argues. Surveys may be used as a forum for potential consumers to express their desires and requirements, which is a fantastic way to attract those who are on the fence about a product or service.

Remember to include social networking functionality as well Whenever appropriate, include "share" buttons for Facebook, Twitter, Google+, and Pinterest. Not only will you improve the number of times your information is shared on social media, but you'll also provide your clients and potential clients with a simple method to share your company's knowledge.

- **Blog.**

Blogging is among the finest methods to interact with consumers. If you actively maintain a high-quality blog, your readers will not only read it but also reply to it. This fosters effective communication and promotes client loyalty.

- **Answer the phone.**

Calling a consumer or client on the phone is the most direct method of communication. There is no better way to develop or enhance a connection than to follow up on a delivery, apologize for anything that went wrong or inquire as to why you haven't gotten an order in a while. Additionally, the phone offers an immediate response in a society dominated by one-way communication.

- **Pay a visit**

The question, "What are your company's most successful channels for consumer involvement both now and in three years? "was posed to marketers in a recent survey. Face-to-face was the most popular choice, given by 59% of respondents. Having said that, it is important to listen to consumers when you visit them rather than immediately attempting to offer them anything.

- **Answer emails.**

'Wow, that was quick or 'Fastest answer I've ever gotten are typical responses we get from our customers when we reach our company's objective of responding to client emails within five minutes. Thank you very much. How does this benefit us? Because of our outstanding customer service, customers are raving about it and suggesting others utilize our service.

- **Send a postcard or letter that is unique to you.**

"I adore using snail mail to send customized cards to my clients to let them know I'm thinking about them,"

These days, physical mail is so scarce that people remember it. Customers feel cherished when they get a card from me because they can see that I put thought and effort into it. Customers purchase and recommend their friends when they feel appreciated.

- **Be active on Facebook and Twitter**.

Social media is one of the finest methods to interact with consumers.

Instead of waiting for consumers to contact you by phone or email with comments, you can instantly connect with them on social media. Utilize the Facebook fan page or Twitter account for your business to interact with your fans and maintain dialogues. Customers may also be served via social media, where corporate employees can respond to their inquiries and grievances immediately.

"Having a social media listening post is essential for promptly responding to any issues that emerge."

Even if you are unable to assist someone with their particular issue, don't disregard them. They'll respect you more since you paid attention to them and recognized their predicament.

Similarly, participating in Twitter parties with the event hashtag is a terrific method to meet clients at trade exhibitions and events.

Share your advice and quotations from the speakers on Twitter, as well as communicate with other people who are also tweeting. Why is this significant, and how can it improve your relationship with potential clients? One, it makes you seem to be an authority on the topic, and two, it introduces you to possible clients you may contact later.

- **Employ Instagram**

Instagram enables us to maintain contact and interaction with our clients and supporters.

We may routinely upload photos, information, competitions, and freebies," the woman claims. "We urge our fans to repost and hashtag to join our competitions and prizes. "When our followers tag us, we may go to their postings and leave comments as well. We can share fresh images and articles related to our brand regularly, and it's been a terrific way to communicate with our followers.

- **Provide webinars**

Webinars or lectures provided online, are a fantastic way to maintain the spice in your client relationships. "Invite a well-known speaker in your field to deliver on a subject your clients want to hear to attract their attention," advises one marketer.

- **Give salesmen authority**

The shopping experience may be made or broken by the salespeople. Giving them real-time access to information and answers that go beyond what they can get online adds value and encourages repeat business. The hallmark of the brick-and-mortar experience is the creation of highly individualized experiences via concierge-like services and professional guidance. In actuality, salespeople are underutilized store assets.

- **Offer superb client service**

"An organization's personnel base is one of its most potent communication channels with consumers.

Every customer-employee encounter, whether it is during the pre-sale, real sales process, after-sales support, or invoicing, offers a chance to either increase or decrease the equity of your brand and business. The relationship between customer satisfaction and loyalty and staff engagement and satisfaction is well supported by empirical data. Making your workers brand ambassadors and company ambassadors who uphold your brand promise and business plan at every single customer contact point are therefore one of the finest methods to engage and connect with consumers.

- **Move about**

Today, almost everyone is carrying a mobile device of some kind—92 percent of Americans own one. Additionally, sending SMS/text messages is a quick, affordable, and tried-and-true method of communication that every mobile phone user is familiar with and can utilize.

According to her, text messaging is a simple method for small companies to engage with their clients since it allows one to contact practically anybody at any time and anywhere in the globe within seconds.

What better approach to engage devoted customers than with a customized app that incorporates location technology and enables automated, targeted message delivery to people close to stores? Location-aware applications provide a whole new avenue for direct communication between consumers and businesses before, during, and after a shopping trip.

- **Keep track of review sites**

Find out what clients are saying about your company [on review sites], whether it be Yelp.

Responding to client complaints on these well-known websites demonstrates that your business is aware of any issues and eager to address them, according to Parkin. She advises prudence when responding to unfavorable remarks, however. Try to comprehend the issue and offer to remedy it, or give a perk to get the consumer to try your product, service, or location again, rather than becoming defensive or beginning a quarrel.

Chapter 3

Boosting Sales by Adding Value

It takes skill to figure out the ideal strategy to boost sales. Many entrepreneurs are concerned about boosting their prices. After all, why wouldn't customers just purchase the lowest item they could find? Not necessarily. You can boost your sales if you know how to use emotional, social, and philosophical principles. You may effectively advertise your items for a higher price by highlighting how beneficial your products are to your target buyers in one of these three key areas.

Knowledge of Emotional Value

Emphasizing the emotional advantages of the purchase is a terrific technique to convince a prospective customer to buy your product rather than one that may be less expensive. Customers want to purchase products that will favorably impact them, and you may convince them that yours will.

This kind of emotional value lets customers recognize that they would much prefer to buy a product that improves or makes them happy than the less expensive alternative that may not necessarily evoke these emotions. For instance, rather than focusing just on how firm or comfy a mattress is, prospective consumers are more likely to choose one that encourages a happier lifestyle as a result of better sleep.

What emotional advantages does your product provide your customers? Find one or two, and be sure to highlight them in your emails, advertisements, and website.

Understanding Social Values

Improve your copywriting and your grasp of the social worth of your product to increase sales. When discussing how other people see your consumers after they have purchased your goods or used your service, social value comes into play. Do they aspire to resemble that individual? Do they value that person's perspective? It doesn't always have to be someone they know; often, just seeing a picture of a stranger who resembles them in appearance and behavior is sufficient.

This factor is usually favorable and may increase sales by raising public awareness. After all, people may seek out your company or brand if they believe that your goods and services are of high quality merely because others have bought them.

Real customer testimonial films are an effective approach to increasing your social worth. Authentic social influencers are another. It also works well for consumers to promote your product on social media in this way, acting as brand ambassadors.

Using philosophic principles

The last thing that company owners should know is what philosophical ideals mean. Philosophical values arise when clients purchase your goods and services to contribute to a better society. They agree with your stance on the issue and support your decision to base your company's operations around it.

Anything might be the source of this sensation. The mere mention of empowerment or optimism in your marketing message or brand voice may be enough to convince a prospective client to buy what you're selling. Your product description or copywriting's explanation of your enthusiasm might be all you need to persuade prospective consumers.

Why did you start your business? What were you hoping to change or make better for other people? Use blog articles, newsletters, and social media to spread this message. Think about launching a charitable initiative that both you and your clients can support.

Chapter 4

Creating a Powerful Product Presentation

Whether you're running a small or large business, product presentations are a big deal. You've probably invested time and resources in creating a fantastic product to solve a market need.

That's great, but presenting your product to investors, prospects and other relevant stakeholders is the final piece of the puzzle.

Weeks, months, and years of research, planning, design, production, and testing often lead up to this point. So, you've got to create a persuasive product presentation that drives sales for your product.

What is a Product Presentation and Why is It Important?

Product presentation is the process of introducing a new or rebranded product to your audience. During product presentations, you'll dig deep into how your product works, how it will address customer pain points, and the specific benefits it will bring to them.

It often involves using visual aids like videos, images, and slideshows to describe product features, benefits, market fit, and other relevant details.

Presentations could take place at different stages of the product development process. But when introducing the product to potential buyers, the stakes are never higher. Therefore it's crucial to make your product presentation effective, impactful, and memorable

In many organizations, product presentations happen at different levels. For example, top management and executives could unveil a new line of products to the board of directors, investors, and potential partners.

Product managers may present a beta or gamma version of a new product to the entire team. In addition, the sales team would have to make product presentations during sales visits to prospects.

Why Create Product Presentations?

There are tons of competing products in the market like yours. Your competitors could be offering similar products or substitutes.

This means that creating useful products may not be enough to set your brand apart or bring in sales. You need product presentations that produce eureka moments for your audience.

Getting it right with your presentations will not only win over your audience, but it'll drive product sales over the top.

But that's just the tip of the iceberg when it comes to the benefits of creating product presentations.

Here are other reasons why you need to create and deliver powerful product presentations.

Create a Memorable First Impression

Nowadays, people are faced with an explosion of product choices. This and many more factors have also contributed to their shrinking attention span.

By any chance, your product presentation could be the first interaction an investor, prospect, or customer has with your brand. So, you have to make it count.

Your product presentation is an excellent opportunity for you to introduce your product and expand their knowledge about your brand. And nailing it will leave a positive and memorable first impression on your audience.

Best of all, it will nudge them to the consideration and conversion stage of your marketing funnel.

Build Trust and Long-Lasting Client Relationships

Customers will buy and recommend brands that provide incredible product and service experiences.

But how do you communicate value and product offerings to your prospects? How do you tilt customer purchase decisions in your favor?

The golden secret is a product presentation that makes you stand out. How you present your product can influence customers' perceptions of your brand.

During product presentations, you have a chance to showcase product features and promise value to clients. And when done right, it can ignite a solid business relationship between you and potential customers.

Over time, these customers will trust your product and become loyal to your brand.

Here's what you should know. As a business owner, brand loyalty, customer trust, and credibility are your greatest assets. A captivating product presentation will inspire client trust in your product and business.

Stand Out from the Competition

The business world is marked by fierce competition among companies that provide similar products and services.

You probably have a lot of competitors and you're wondering how to distinguish yourself. Start by delivering a flawless product presentation.

As previously stated, your sales presentation should be able to leave an indelible impression on prospects and investors. It would captivate their attention so completely that, regardless of the stiff competition, they would always opt for your brand.

Boost Sales and Revenue

Having an excellent presentation is the key that unlocking sales for your product.

After your presentation, you certainly want customers to pull out their checks or proceed to the next steps. If you can nail your product presentations, you will win over your audience, gain new customers and increase sales.

On the contrary, mediocre product presentations could hurt your brand. You might even have a top product that has the potential to be a major game-changer. But poor delivery would not only portray you as lacking confidence in your product but could be a turn-off for prospects.

Product Presentation vs. Sales Presentation

Product presentations aren't so different from sales pitches. Both presentations focus on providing value or solutions to customers. However, product presentations are primarily focused on products or services.

With product presentations, you'll dive deeper into details like:

How your product works

How it will solve your customer's needs or pain points

The specific benefits your product will bring to your customers

For instance, sales presentations can have a broad focus on your business as a whole rather than a particular product.

Let's say you run an accounting firm that offers a wide range of products and services. Your sales presentations could focus on pitching solutions like:

Accounting audit
Tax accounting
Bookkeeping
Forensic Accounting

On the flip side, you'll need a product presentation to sell inventory management or accounting software to your clients.

Keep in mind that both presentations are essential for your sales process. The goal is to get your prospects' attention, drum up excitement and move them toward making a purchase decision.

What You Need in a Product Presentation

Although product presentations cut across different industries, there's no universally accepted format. However, this infographic template below highlights the key elements of winning a product presentation.

- Introduction
- Company Overview
- The Problem
- Product and Solution
- The promise of Value or Benefits
- Product Positioning

- Use Cases and Social Proof
- Call-to-Action
- Conclusion

Together, these key details juice up your product presentation and make it a delight for your audience.

Introduction

The introductory part is where you hook your audience in and get them excited about your presentation. It should provide an overview of what you will cover during your presentation.

In this section, you can sum up the purpose of your presentation, why it's relevant to your audience, and key takeaways.

Company Overview

Before you get into the product details, start with a general overview of your company. It doesn't matter if your audience is familiar with your business or not. You want to include key details such as:

Company name
Vision, mission, and goals
When your business was created
The products and services you offer
How your business and products have evolved
Relevant team members

The Problem

The problem or customer needs should receive more attention than others. This is what your prospects care about most and that's why they are sitting at the other end of the table. So we recommend that you include this section earlier in the presentation.

To attract the audience's attention, show them you have an in-depth understanding of pain points. Remember to explain how the problem affects your audience and the consequences of not resolving it.

Product and Solution

Start by showing your audience how they'll feel or what they could enjoy if they solve that problem. Here, you want to paint a mental picture of a perfect world without those pain points.

While writing this section, be sure to highlight these things:

Introduce your product or service.

Briefly explain how it addresses the problem and makes their dream of a perfect world a reality.

Highlight how your product is made. Is it handcrafted, mass-produced, custom-made, or batch produced?

Include product details like features, functionalities, specifications, durability, quality, and more.

Promise of Value

No product presentation is complete without a value proposition. This is where you make a case for your product. Articulating your promise of value will help create an "aha moment" for your prospects.

This section should provide more insight into the value your product Is offering. Here you should:

Mention what your audience will get out of the product (product or service experience)

Highlight what makes your product unique from other competing products (unique selling proposition)

Explain why your prospect should opt for your product (competitive edge)

It's a good idea to center your product pitch around the key benefits your prospects will enjoy. So you want to highlight as many product benefits as possible. It could be productivity, convenience, health and wellness, peace of mind, and much more.

Product Positioning

Product positioning refers to how you want your market to think or feel about your product. It's a description of who you are as a brand, the products and services you offer, your target market, and what makes your product unique.

Here you should talk about:

Your brand image and values

The positioning of competing products in your target market

How your product features and benefits stack up to the competition

Brand positioning helps to set you apart from your competitors. Think of it as what customers can remember about your brand when they think of similar products.

For example, the Pepsi brand is distinct from the Coca-Cola brand. Even though they are both cola drinks, they have different tastes, looks, connotations, and legacies.

To influence customers' perceptions of your brand, you could create a brand positioning statement. For example, a recent marketing campaign by Salesforce highlights their brand positioning statement:

We bring companies and customers together. We make technology that supercharges every part of your company that connects with customers, delivering a 360-degree customer view across sales, marketing, service, e-commerce, mobile apps, connected products, and more. CRM also powers integration with all the other parts of your business already humming along, including supply chains and finance, its back office, front office, and offices yet to come.

Use Cases and Social Proof

This section should provide a visual picture of the customer using your product to address their problems. Here are some ways you can visualize or share them in your presentation.

Create a scenario of how customers can use your product to solve their problems.

Share customer reviews, testimonials, user ratings, celebrity endorsements, expert reviews, and more.

Share case studies and real results of how your product has helped similar businesses.

Provide a snapshot of your product performance in terms of downloads, engagements, purchases, and much more.

Mention any product and compliance certifications, documentation, quality badges, and awards you've received.

Use anecdotes to showcase how existing customers love your solution.

Call-to-Action (CTA)

Now it's time to tell your viewers what you expect from them. Your call to action will depend on your audience.

It will also depend on the goal of your product presentations, which we'll discuss in the next section.

During in-house product presentations, you might want to ask for feedback from different departments. At a trade show, you might ask to meet prospective customers to meet you at the booth to make purchases.

During B2B presentations, you might request a time for questions and more. Ultimately the goal is to get customers to purchase your product.

How to Create a Powerful Product Presentation in 10 Steps

Most businesses have confidence in their ability to make excellent products. However, they struggle to commercialize or bring in revenues from those products.

Why's that? The attention spans of people in this tech-driven society are shrinking. And the reality is that people no longer have enough time to sit through mediocre product presentations.

Want to drive sales or get a positive return on investment for your product? Then you've got to make your product presentations compelling.

Let me show you how to create compelling product presentations that capture the important elements I've highlighted above.

- **Define Your Goals**

Whether you're presenting a new, rebranded, or upgraded product, the first thing you need to do is to define your goals and objectives.

Let's say you've launched a new line of products into the market. Firstly, you'll have to spell out what you're looking to achieve with your product presentation.

Do you want to get investors' buy-in to expand production capacity?

Do you want to secure more funding from management to produce more units?

Are you looking to secure partnerships with distributors, retailers, or franchisees? Or you want to introduce the new product to your prospects or client.

Secondly, reiterate why it's important for you and your team to achieve these goals. For example, as you'd expect, securing partnerships with distributors could help:

Expand your product reach
Boost product sales and revenue
Increase market share and more

Next, you want to highlight how you intend to communicate with your audience. Also, be clear about what you want your audience to do after watching your presentation.

Do you want your prospects to call you or buy one year's supply of your product? What about in-house presentations? Do you want the sales and marketing team to develop a strategy to introduce the product into a new market? Your presentations should convincingly answer these questions.

It makes sense, right? Lastly, remember to make your goals specific, measurable, attainable, realistic, and time-bound (SMART).

The success of your presentation is measured by whether your audience understands and acts on your message. Therefore consider your goals in every slide and include a clear call to action.

- **Figure Out What Your Audience Needs**

If you want to pique your audience's interest in your product, you'll have to figure out what matters most to them and serve it to them. This is what sets successful brands apart.

Don't make the mistake of assuming you know what your target audience wants, which is a trap many businesses fall into. Rather go ahead and do these things:

- Perform in-depth research into your audience
- Develop buyer personas
- Delve into customer data to monitor patterns or trends
- Keep an eye on social media, public forums, and industry publications

We get it. You've probably gone through this process during product development. Now you're wondering why it matters during the presentation.

Here's what you should know. Getting access to information is much easier than ever. As a result, potential buyers extensively research products and scan competitors' offerings before making purchases.

So your presentation is an opportunity to demonstrate that you not only understand their pain points, but your products can make their life or business better.

- **Create an Outline**

The next step is to outline the main points you want to hit during your presentation.

During presentations, there are usually a lot of key points to cover. Creating an outline helps you ensure things don't fall through the cracks.

First, decide the topics you want to cover and the sequence to present them. Then dedicate a slide to show the outline to your audience. This will give them an idea of what to expect and make your delivery insightful.

- **Pick Out the Right Tool and Template**

Presenting your product or services is an art. You need a rich blend of visually appealing slides and powerful delivery to make it effective.

Achieving this may require long hours of planning, strategy, design, and organization. You'd have to craft an outline, prepare your slide notes, source royalty-free visuals, and use them to design your slides.

- **Make Your Content Relevant and Compelling**

Creating relevant and convincing content is the key to nailing your product presentation.

The other ideas we've shared will make your content more effective. But an excellent presentation begins and ends with great content. It has the potential to capture the hearts and minds of viewers and connect them with your solution.

Don't just assume you can wing it by putting less effort into developing compelling content. You'll need to spend a lot of time researching, brainstorming, and writing out the key points relevant to your audience.

For example, some customers may care more about product quality than price.

On the other hand, convenience and ease of use could be primary concerns for other prospects.

While your presentation should be brief, the value proposition should be at the heart of your sales pitch. You want to focus on how the product will benefit the customer rather than the aesthetics.

Start by describing the world your customers will enjoy after purchase. And be sure to quickly convey what makes your product different.

For instance, the process of buying and installing new equipment can sometimes be tricky and demanding. But it helps companies bring down costs, and increase productivity and revenue.

Your content should communicate the problem and what the prospect will enjoy after buying your product. Offering additional perks like pre-purchase and after-sales support can further convince customers to buy.

- **Bring Your Presentation to Life With Attractive Designs**

Think about the last time you sat through a dull presentation.

What were the slide designs like?

Was the color scheme dull or monotonous?

Were the visual aids clumsy and difficult to understand?

Were there too many ideas crammed on each slide?

You probably zoned away during the presentation. Like you, other people feel the same way about terrible slide decks.

Regardless of how amazing the quality of your content may be, a poor slide design can be frustrating to watch.

Not only will it hurt your product presentation, but it could undermine your credibility. So, you want to ensure your slide design is not only professional but has a clean and organized layout.

Here's how to get savvy with your slide design.

Use legible fonts and stick with a minimum of three fonts throughout your slide deck.

Avoid using too many colors in your presentation.

Be sure there's a strong contrast between your text color and background color.

Tailor your typography, color scheme, and visual language to your brand identity.

Format your text, images, and design element to achieve perfection.

- **Use High-quality Graphics and Visual Aids**

Incorporating quality visual aids into your product presentation is a must.

Why does it matter? The thing is, you've put a lot of time and effort into preparing for your big day. So you certainly don't want your prospects to leave the room recalling only a tiny fraction of what you said.

According to a study, 65% of people are visual learners. So adding stunning visuals in your presentations ensures the odds are stacked in your favor.

No matter the type of audience you're looking to reach. Impactful visuals help you communicate your message and ideas more effectively. Best of all, they grab and retain audience attention, build solid emotional connections and keep your presentation on track.

Avoid using pixelated or cheesy images. Even more, stay away from generic stock art, copyrighted or watermarked visuals available. Rather source top-quality photos that enhance your presentation.

Just like it's important to stick to one main idea per slide, use one or two images per slide. But, again, the key is to use images that convey your message in the most compelling way possible.

- **Determine Follow-Up Questions and Provide Answers**

At the end of your product presentation, prospects or investors are likely to have a handful of questions about your product.

Typically prospective customers ask questions to know if the product is a right fit for their organization. These questions could be along the lines of:

Scalability
Pricing
Quality assurance
Ease of use
After-sales support and more

For example, let's say you've built a digital product like customer relationship management (CRM) software. Prospects could ask questions such as:

Is your software scalable?

Will it support our company's growth and future expansion plans?

How will the tool help us manage our day-to-day process?

How will the product help our business grow sales, gain a competitive advantage, or increase market share?

Most clients could even ask for a live demo or a trial of your software.

Preparing for potential questions will help you avoid getting caught off-guard. It also shows you clearly understand your prospect's needs.

Answering these questions will wow your audience, boost their confidence in your product, and help you close the deal.

- **Run It by Your Team and Incorporate Feedback**

You've spent time designing your slide and putting your ideas together. Great job. Now your presentation needs a few rounds of edits to make it shine.

Here's how to polish your presentation to make it pop.

Keep editing aggressively until your presentation is clear and free of fluff. The goal is to improve language accuracy, flow, and overall legibility.

Be sure to weed out anything that doesn't relate to the core message.

Run it by your mentor and team members, get their feedback and incorporate it into your product presentation.

Getting a fresh pair of eyes to look at your presentation can help you refine it, even if you're a good editor.

Here's the deal. When editing your presentation, your brain could instinctively fill in the gaps with what you wanted to say. But other editors could readily flag errors or point out areas where you aren't expressing your ideas clearly.

If you don't have anyone within reach, automated writing assistants like Grammarly and ProWritingAid could come in handy.

- **Practice Your Presentation**

If you want to deliver captivating business presentations, rehearse till you become perfect.

Why does it matter anyway? After all, you've gone through the entire product development process and have a good grasp of the product.

Notable speakers like Steve Jobs and Dr. Jill Bolte-Taylor practiced their speeches many times before delivering speeches before getting on stage. And guess what! They nailed it every single time.

Steve Jobs's rehearsal routine and his ability to communicate their ideas persuasively drove massive sales for Apple products. It has also played a vital role in the success of the Apple brand.

Rehearsals grow your confidence and make you familiar with the key points. As you rehearse, you have a great opportunity to:

Weed out the irrelevant points or jargon in your presentations

Try something new (like a strong opening or pause to play a clip)

Streamline your presentations for the allotted time

Practice your product presentations between five to ten times before the big day. You can do it alone (facing the mirror) on the first day.

Then you can practice before a small group of friends, family, and colleagues. This will enable you to see reactions and get natural human feedback.

While you're at it, make sure to time yourself, record your practice sessions and take notes.

Feel free to enunciate tricky words and pause when you notice mistakes. Be sure to analyze, reanalyze and refine your presentation structure as you proceed.

Go ahead and review the recorded clips and feedback from your practice audience. Once done, you can then incorporate the feedback into your remaining practice sessions.

Remember, you shouldn't read your slide or deliver the presentation just the way you memorize it. The goal of rehearsals is to build enough confidence to:

Avoid sounding rigid or too rehearsed

Present your product or services without appearing unprepared

Take questions and comments from your audience without getting lost or overwhelmed

Chapter 5

Increasing average transaction Value

The average amount of money that clients spend each time they purchase from you is referred to as the average transaction value. It is sometimes referred to as the "average transaction," "unit per transaction," "average transaction size," "average transaction value," "average sale per customer," or "average amount per sale."

Your company should ideally be maximizing the value of each sale. You may maximize the value of each transaction by using a variety of selling strategies. You must provide your clients with additional choices, discounts, and bundles. You may maximize each sale by up-selling, cross-selling, and bundling your goods with those of other companies or with their own.

Another option is to just ask the consumer to make a purchase. Take McDonald's as a prime illustration: They developed a straightforward method for raising the average transaction value per customer years ago by asking each client who made a purchase from them, "... and would you be having fries and a drink with your meal today?"

People say "yes" around 30% of the time even though it may not have crossed their minds. The result is a 30% rise in fries or drinks sales and a profit contribution from those lines that is almost 100% higher.

The formula for Average Transaction Value

You may determine the average amount customers spend each time they make a purchase from you by adding up your total sales and dividing it by the number of transactions made. We want to enhance customers' spending each time they purchase from you. We'll monitor your overall sales over a certain period to determine what your average transaction value (in dollars per sale) was. We need to put new techniques into place that will raise this amount to boost your average transaction value or average Dollar per sale. On the other side, it's useful to know which clients spend the most money with you so you can reward these devoted customers and come up with creative methods to keep them coming back.

These are broad tactics that have proven successful for many firms, but not all of them may be the greatest for your unique industry.

Techniques to increase your average transaction value

- Set a goal for the average transaction value:

It's crucial to set a target average transaction value or average dollar sale that everyone in your organization is aware of. Keep an eye on the outcomes so you can adjust your tactics as needed.

- Increase the cost of your goods or services:

By raising your pricing, you may also raise the average transaction value. Compared to a rapid price increase, customers will have less trouble adjusting if tiny, gradual increases are made over time. There are several simple methods to raise prices without driving away clients, and nothing can improve your revenues more quickly than this, but this is not the ideal strategy for increasing your average dollar sale. You might even inform your consumers that the price will increase on a specified day in the future. They must place their purchase right away if they want the item at this pricing.

- Promote value above price:

People purchase advantages and experiences rather than things or features. They purchase the "wonderful sound," the joyful, upbeat emotion they would have, rather than the stereo.

The majority of purchase decisions—more than 80% of them—are driven by emotion. It's crucial to emphasize how your product or service will improve the lives of your consumers. You must be aware of their thoughts.

Connecting your product and service to the wants of your ideal consumer should be straightforward if you have done enough research to identify who they are and what they specifically desire.

How would utilizing your goods or services assist your customers? People pay attention to advantages. People want benefits beyond anything else. The way you explain your advantages to others may make the difference between success and failure. People are curious about their benefits.

- Request further purchases from your existing supporters:

If you don't inquire, you won't find out the response. Ask a client if they would want to purchase an extra item to go along with or some extras to complete the original product the next time you are speaking with a customer. 90% of the time, customers are unaware of all the extras they may add to customize their order. Inform them about your special offers, contests, and product debuts. This is a terrific approach to raising the average transaction value for your business.

McDonald's, for instance, poses the question. And today, will your meal include fries and a beverage? People say "yes" around 30% of the time even though it may not have crossed their minds. The result is a 30% rise in sales of beverages and fries and an increase in profit contribution from those segments of the business of almost 100%.

- Don't permit a discount:

Giving a discount to clinch a transaction is not always a good idea; instead, provides an incentive. Discounting will lower your profit margin as well as sales revenue and average transaction value. Instead, raise the value of your product or service to boost average transaction value, revenue, and profitability.

- Sell more of your goods or services:

Make sure that the consumer is satisfied with the purchase before trying to upsell (sell them more) your goods or services to them. Sell your consumers a more expensive, higher-quality item or an upgraded version of your product or service. Sell a less-priced product if cost and budget are your main concerns.

Give customers a range of prices, colors, sizes, and forms to choose from. This is a fantastic tactic for raising average transaction value. Additionally, you may urge consumers to make larger purchases. Recall how the query "Do you want fries with that?" generates 18% of McDonald's overall sales. So figure out how to apply the same concept to your company. This may be accomplished originally with a thank-you card, catalog, phone call, or one-time offer.

- Cross-selling or up-selling on additional goods or services:

Cross-selling is the practice of promoting other things that clients may be interested in purchasing depending on the original items in which they have shown interest. To entice customers before they leave your business, you might place impulsive purchases next to complementary products or display images of them at the payment point.

Sell extra items to consumers that support or enhance the good or service. For instance, if you offer your client soap, sell an attractive container or a refill package along with it. Try to sell some washers together with the bolts you are selling your customers. Use other companies' goods together with your own if that is what it takes.

- Reduce the price of goods or services:

The consumer will believe that the product or service they had in mind was inexpensive if you provide them with the more costly version of your offering before the less expensive one.

- Utilize checklists:

Check a checklist before a buyer purchases anything to make sure they won't need anything else. Ask the purchaser whether they will need dog food, a blanket, dog shampoo, and maybe a brush if they get a puppy. Make sure your checklist fits all of your goods and services.

- Use questionnaires:

Give your consumers survey forms with questions on them so they may let you know what they want. You will learn more about their needs and desires the more they can communicate with you. You can meet their wants and determine what else to market to them using this quiz. To touch your consumers' hearts, use inventiveness.

When selling, use either-or questions:

A consumer is more inclined to purchase when given an option. Asking the buyer about their preferred color, delivery date, and payment method will provide them with an option. It's a successful method of completing a deal.

'Ask me' tools may be buttons:

Using buttons to encourage clients to inquire about special deals is both affordable and effective. Additionally, they might open the door for staff members to pitch other goods and services. Use buttons that are customized to certain specials or a generic button that says, "Ask me about today's deal."

Utilize the phone to upsell:

Try to pull a "Columbo" after the operator has accepted the order: Oh, just one more thing. Would you want to learn about our exclusive offer for today's callers? Or Just one more thing: Would you want to learn about our exclusive extra-special offer for today's callers?

Use persuasive sales scripts:

Every sales call is an excellent chance for you to deepen your connection with the caller. Your phone should always be answered professionally and in the same manner. If you have to put the clients on wait, you may play a message promoting your business or product or informing them of a current promotion.

Provide options:

Offer your customer the more costly item or service first, followed by the cheaper one. Show the best product to your buyer first. Inform your consumer of the characteristics, advantages, and special attributes of this product. If the customer's budget does not allow for the higher-priced item, it would be best to demonstrate how the product operates before selling them the less expensive option.

Present the finest offer, not the cheapest one:

Describe the advantages of your item or service and how they may assist the buyer in making a purchase choice. People purchase to satisfy their needs; they don't always choose the cheapest good or service.

Pareto's law, sometimes known as the 80/20 rule:

Essentially, Pareto's Law states that around 20% of the stock will account for 80% of the total turnover. This ratio applies to all industries, including the service industry, and is a reliable way to raise the average transaction value. Consequently, begin by classifying your product or service into:

A - The best-selling items or the 20% or so of the total goods or services supplied that account for 80% or more of the total because of greater gross margins.
B - The typical sellers, who make up around 30% of the overall stock and contribute 10% or so to sales.
C - The poor sellers, which make up around 50% of the inventory and provide 10% or less to sales or profits.

These percentages may vary from company to company and industry to industry, but the general idea tends to stay true. The "A" items, or winners, are the most significant since they account for the majority of sales (and profit as well), and therefore should always be in stock. Poor selling "C" items don't sell in large quantities, thus they don't need to be well supplied. In time, they may even be phased out in favor of a better selling line.

Keep more expensive goods in stock:

Provide higher-margin goods for people who may ask for them and have the funds to do so. But be certain that it will sell. You may use the good, better, best product approach, in which you provide the buyer with three pricing alternatives and let them choose. Customers often choose the middle choice. This will significantly alter your average transaction value.

Diversify:

extend the range of your items and your horizons. You'll automatically provide your clients and potential clients with more alternatives. Sales will increase as a result of this.

Offer fresh, cutting-edge goods:

Offer new products to your increasing consumer base sometimes.

Offer only high-quality goods and services:

Discover how your consumer defines quality since that is what they are prepared to pay for. Promote value addition and quality above pricing.

Quality commands a higher price, so you can charge more and make more money.

Carry a curated selection of goods or services:

You ensure you are the only one with it by selling your own carefully chosen line of goods. There won't be any rivals, and customers will only purchase from you if they want or desire the product or service you provide. One, you own the market, and two, you don't have any rivals to go off against. You may also ask your clients what modifications they would like to see or what new developments they are looking for, then use that information for your brand-new product or service.

Close collaborations with other businesses:

By promoting and selling each other's goods and services, joint ventures with other connected but non-competitive enterprises help to grow transaction size. As long as they are connected in some manner and complement one another, this may work effectively. For instance, a business that sells printers could also offer stationery or copy paper. You'll be able to raise the average sale as a result.

Reorganize the merchandise and layout of your store:

Customers must find your place of business appealing in terms of both the overall design and image. There must be sufficient walking room, a clean appearance, and clear directions to everything. Shelves need to be densely packed and well-stocked.

Bring in more customers for your items by:

The consumer may be informed about the product on a particular shelf, its characteristics and advantages, and what accessories go with it through a vibrant display on each shelf. For smaller items, use bin labels to provide the color, size, and description so that buyers can find them quickly. Your customers must be drawn to your items.

Let people make impulsive purchases:

This is extremely effective in raising average transaction value! Place treats or magazines next to the counters where clients must pay. The more they observe and the more likely they are to make a purchase, the longer they wait. effectively employed in settings where moms are accompanied by their children or in clothes shops where women may peruse the newest publications. For the innovative ones, go outside the box and put unusual or humorous items—attractive items—near the counter or in a prominent location where your clients will not miss them!

Add fees for extra services:

Add-on services like your time and expertise should be priced more. People will have more faith in you since you seem more professional if you charge for your time and expertise because it will give your product or service more legitimacy. The advantage of just receiving folks who are serious about your product or service is another benefit.

Increase the average transaction value by bundling:

Combine extras into a single, affordable bundle. Include a special bundle pricing that can only be gotten by buying the original item to add to the temptation. Add a lower value premium to a major item or service if sales aren't strong. Pick an item that fits with the general topic of your advertising campaign or promotion. This will increase the drink campaign's in-store effectiveness.

A complimentary branded energy drink and a protein bar, for instance, would be an excellent approach to increase your average dollar sale if you were advertising sportswear. Choose products that your clients are likely to find appealing. What is currently trending and new? Things that benefit the charity may be quite effective. 95% of consumers say they would keep doing business with a firm if they think it supports the community. 68% of consumers think that they will spend more money on a product if it supports a worthy cause. Invest in a fundraiser item from a charity and sell it in bulk to your clients.

Offer your contracts for customer service:

If you are selling a product, request that the buyer sign a service agreement with you for the duration of the agreement. Ask for a contract if you are selling consumables so the buyer will utilize you for a certain amount of time. Just keep in mind to provide fast and effective service. No matter what you have to offer, strive to get your consumer to commit for a while; who knows? They could end up becoming lifetime fans!

Deliveries may be added as an extra:

This is the ideal strategy to use if you want to raise your average dollar sale. By bringing the goods to the customer's home, you first make it simpler for them to purchase the product from you and you also make more money. For a little cost, you may also offer to wrap and send clients' purchases.

Charge for any additional services you may offer:

Charge for sending out monthly newsletters, packages, and membership in a club where customers get additional pamphlets or news. Offer a service wherein you send the client's package on their behalf to the recipient they choose (like flowers).

Offer discounted prices:

Give discounts to businesses that purchase in large quantities or to people who purchase more often than the majority of other consumers.

When you spend a particular amount, provide a gift:

Reward the consumer if their purchase exceeds a specified threshold. Customers will be inspired to spend more money when they visit your shop as a result.

Create discounts for large purchases:

Promote a discount if a consumer makes a high number of purchases. By doing this, the consumer will save money, get used to using your product or service, and come back when supplies are low again. Additionally, it will boost your average transaction value and help you sell more.

Increase the value of your goods or services:

Giving your consumers anything for free will increase the value of a sale for them. When they make their first buy, offer them an additional product, and after their fifth transaction, give them a service for free. In other words, you're adding value by giving it away.

Provide more for a higher transaction value:

Increase the value of your goods and services to entice customers to make more purchases. Add other services or goods on top of the one the client is purchasing. In the end, the buyer does pay more, but they get a better deal. Promote the value you are providing to the consumer.

When making an order, establish a minimum amount:

You must establish a minimum order quantity to cover travel costs while maintaining a profit. Your shipping costs will also be covered by this.

Give a discount for purchases beyond a particular amount:

Give clients a reward, discount, or points when they spend a specific amount and more. Just keep in mind to increase it by 20% from your current average dollar sale.

Run promotions like buy one, get one free one:

This is a fantastic approach to get rid of the outdated inventory you have on your shelf but simply can't seem to part with! You may use it to introduce a new product to your clients, ensuring that you don't run the danger of losing sales just because they are unfamiliar with it. However, using goods with a fair markup is the best option; just be sure to verify with your vendors first.

Create bundles where you sell two or more items for the price of one of the profit margin permits. People will purchase more than normal if they believe they won't get another deal like it. Just make sure you can still turn a profit with your markup.

Provide an additional warranty or insurance for your products:

Inquire about your clients' interest in purchasing an additional warranty or insurance for the item they have already paid for. Greater transactions and larger average transactions result from this.

Offer simple payment options:

Give your consumers simple payment options, such as credit cards, debit cards, cash, or checks. By doing this, you make it simpler for them to spend more money than they had originally intended.

Acceptable conditions for financing or payment

You should take the effort to divide your pricing, no matter how low it may be, into even smaller quantities. You may remark, "That's merely five little payments of R200 each," if the cost of what you sell is R1000. Your goods and services will become more inexpensive as a result. Mentioning the fact that you take all payment cards is another method to go about it.

Permit product exchanges between customers:

Change an outdated item for a new one, or an older model for a newer one, with a discounted price for the new item for the consumer. The previous item may then be sold to a different client or business.

Give them the option to lay buy:

Paying in installments allows you to purchase items now and pay the remaining balance later. This is a fantastic solution for folks who can't pay the full price today to get the goods they truly desire more inexpensively. Additionally, you have the opportunity to encounter them more often in your shop for payment and maybe additional sales.

Create a trusting connection with your customers:

Asking your consumers questions and paying close attention to their answers can help you develop connections and trust with them. Call them by name and use their "language." You should be able to provide your customers with appropriate guidance and support on your goods and services if you are familiar with them. You will be able to reassure them that they made the right choice by showing them how your good or service is the solution to their issue or need.

Make sure your client is knowledgeable:

Make sure your consumer is aware of all the products and services you provide. What you offer and how you sell it must be crystal clear to your consumers. Keep them informed of new developments and adjustments. Never presume they are aware of your whole product line before introducing it to them. Because consumers often forget, remind them.

Offer a list of products or services:

What you offer and how you sell it must be crystal clear to your consumers. Keep them informed of new developments and adjustments. Never presume they are aware of your whole product line before introducing it to them. Because consumers often forget, remind them. Give them a list of the products, their characteristics, and the costs.

Educate and inform your clients to spend more money:

You must inform your clients about your goods and services as well as the way your organization operates. In addition to that, you must provide outstanding customer service to keep your clients coming back. Follow up often to stay in contact with them and sometimes provide feedback.

Conduct ongoing promotions:

To raise average transaction value, run frequent promotions in your business on your goods or services. Run promotions like offers, add-ons, product demos, or a celebrity engaging customers throughout open hours. Because they will be on the lookout for the next special deal, you won't only draw in new clients; you'll also retain the ones you already have. earning money and enjoying yourself! Consider how you may make contests meaningful.

Prioritize value above price:

When describing your goods or services to customers, put value first rather than price. A product's qualities and advantages should be its primary concern, not its cost. By highlighting the ease and happiness that will result from the customer's purchase of your goods, you may draw their attention to such qualities. People accept advantages. A higher average transaction value results from more advantages and value.

Give the sales crew enough incentives and training:

The most crucial members of a corporation are the salesmen. When a consumer enters your store, they will interact with those individuals. These individuals will be crucial to your sales. Your care for them will determine what they know, how they move and speak, how they seem, and how they treat clients. Set sales goals and objectives, provide them with the training they need, reward them, and make them feel special.

Build on professionalism, quality, and image:

Maintain a polished demeanor at all times. Make sure everyone on your staff is well-groomed and your shop is clean and tidy. Verify that your cars are well-maintained, clearly labeled with your company's brand and tagline, and clean. Teach your employees to put the needs of the client first while maintaining pride in their job and environment. You will project an image of quality and superiority as a result.

Give your employees, cars, and shop a high-quality, professional appearance. Dress and conduct yourself well. By doing this, you will draw in customers who are more intelligent and have the resources to buy pricey and lucrative things, which will increase the average transaction value.

Giving sales teams bonuses for higher sales:

When sales goals are fulfilled, provide your salespeople bonuses or significant incentives (make it something they truly desire). Maintaining a positive attitude will result in tremendous sales. Set goals and incentives for salespeople to raise the minimum average transaction value.

Only choose clients who are worth the effort:

Select your consumers by only providing service to those who are worth the effort. Create groups from your consumer base. One group will be the more lucrative and hassle-free consumers, while the other group will be the folks you need to educate about how your company works and what you want from them.

Get rid of expensive clients:

Make it very obvious to this kind of consumer how your company does business and what you anticipate from them. These are the clients who are the most demanding, who pay slowly, and who use most of your time and resources. Eliminate them! At the end of the day, they cost you more.

Reward devoted customers with extra consideration:

When a devoted consumer spends more than the typical transaction amount, reward them favorably. Receiving free goods or services, exclusive deals that aren't accessible to other consumers, and exclusive privileges are just a few examples of this exceptional treatment. Retail has long offered stamp or bonus point schemes.

Chapter 6

Invest in yourself as a Business owner

Startup business owners often work all by themselves or almost all by themselves. They combine the skills of idea generators, ardent leaders, team builders, engineers, marketing specialists, logistics officers, bookkeepers, and strategists.

The truth is that this phase is often required. This implies that continuing to invest and continue to develop one's own unique set of talents and abilities is one of the startup-most minded's difficult tasks. It's a huge struggle in terms of time and effort. The majority of company owners avoid making personal investments because they feel they are unrelated to their operations and goods. For instance, many business owners would rather invest in their firm than in themselves if they had an additional hour.

The issue with that strategy is that the majority of business owners are also their brands and goods.

Furthermore, it makes business sense to make sure that those shoulders are as prepared, as competent, and as powerful as possible if you can step back and realize that your whole entrepreneurial endeavor relies on a single pair of shoulders. As a result, you must invest in yourself as doing so is equivalent to investing in your service or product.

Entrepreneurs sometimes don't know where to begin since they spend so little time thinking about developing their talents and abilities while focusing on their company. I have some ideas on how you may continue investing in yourself even if you're a stressed-out entrepreneur since I've spent much of my professional life at the nexus of business and education.

- **Attend school**

Higher education is one of the best ways to build your reputation and intellectual aptitude. The learning setting itself may foster creativity and open up new connections. Today, every city has incubators that provide specialized training. A major difference may be made by completing your degree or beginning a new one, and almost every institution offers a part-time, returning student, or executive program.

- **Teach**

If you're a teacher, a school setting has equal authority. Moreover, having teaching experience lends a lot of credibilities, similar to that of a graduate degree. Additionally, teaching pushes you to think critically about new concepts, face old ones, and present information in fresh ways. Get involved in the classroom if you are an expert in a subject by getting in touch with local universities or community learning initiatives.

- **online course**

While there is still a buyer-beware mentality in the online learning environment, more and more reputable universities and incubators are providing online courses and programs. From institutions like Harvard, Stanford, or any number of state colleges, you may get credentials in a range of business-related fields. It's a wise investment, even if you're merely challenging your intellect or keeping up with current events and trends.

If you like reading, make sure your reading list contains subjects that have nothing to do with your professional activities. Whatever may divert your attention from your hourly obsessions, such as crime thrillers, romantic novels, or theoretical physics, should be read. The ability to think creatively and problem-solve will increase when you take a break from your job. Reading about ants or Adam Ant for only a few hours each week may have a significant impact.

- **Physical wellbeing**

One of the greatest mistakes business owners make is to disregard their physical well-being. It makes no sense to take a chance with your ability to work if it's the most important factor in your company's success. I am aware of how difficult it is, but go to the gym and choose a healthy diet. Go on vacation. As with all of these recommendations, it may be helpful to see maintaining good health as an investment in your company.

- **Co-working**

Think about relocating your company and yourself to a coworking environment. It may be addictive and motivating to work together in an entrepreneurial culture of shared desire and sacrifice. By co-locating, you may meet mentors, partners, and unconventional thinkers who can all contribute to your strategic inventiveness and personal development.

- **Network**

Participate in groups and activities. Most individuals perceive networking as a chance to develop their enterprises. However, they are equally crucial for developing relationships that you can carry with you from job to job or company to business. You may expand your reach and capability by making an investment in networking and getting to know your network on a personal level.

www.ingramcontent.com/pod-product-compliance
Lightning Source LLC
LaVergne TN
LVHW010611160826
845677LV00013B/3359

* 9 7 9 8 8 4 9 9 8 3 4 2 4 *